Hal•Leonard
EASY
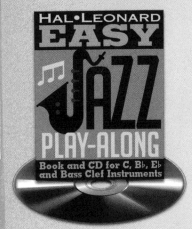
JAZZ
PLAY-ALONG
Book and CD for C, Bb, Eb
and Bass Clef Instruments

Volume 5

EASY LATIN CLASSICS

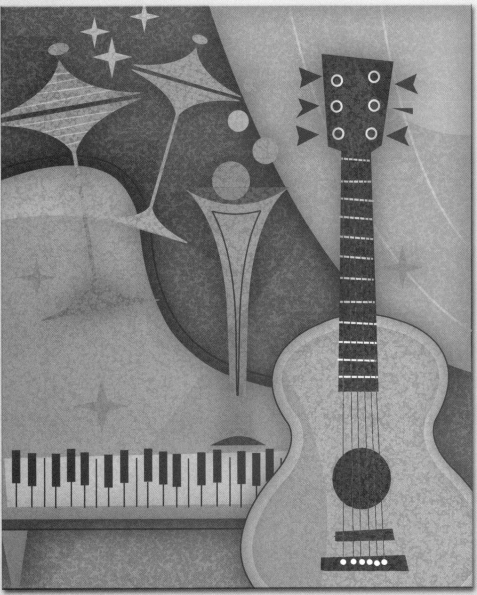

Recorded by Ric Probst at Tanner Monagle Studio
Piano: Mark Davis
Bass: Tom McGirr
Drums: Dave Bayles

ISBN 978-1-4768-0195-7

HAL•LEONARD®
CORPORATION
7777 W. BLUEMOUND RD. P.O. BOX 13819 MILWAUKEE, WI 53213

Visit Hal Leonard Online at
www.halleonard.com

CONTENTS

BOOK

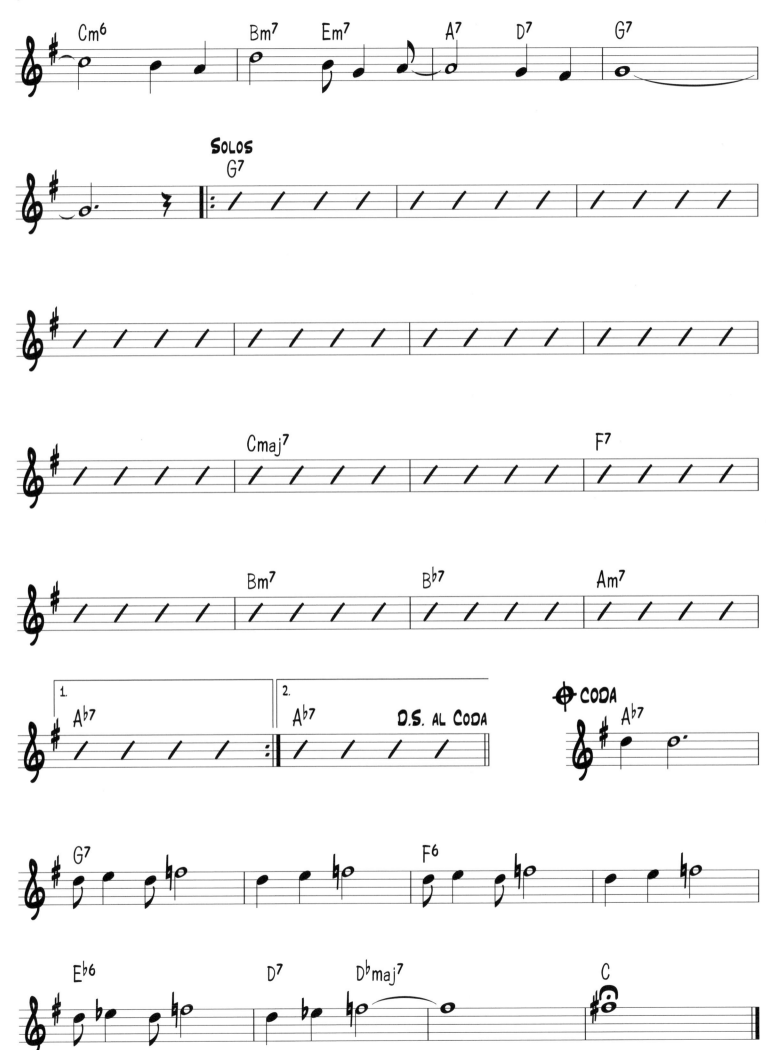

BAIA
(Bahia)

C VERSION

Music and Portuguese Lyric by Ary Barroso
English Lyric by Ray Gilbert

CONTENTS

CD

Begin the Beguine

C Version

Words and Music by
Cole Porter

9

Black Orpheus

C Version

Words and Music by Luiz Bonfa
and Antonio Carlos Jobim

Introduction
Medium Bossa

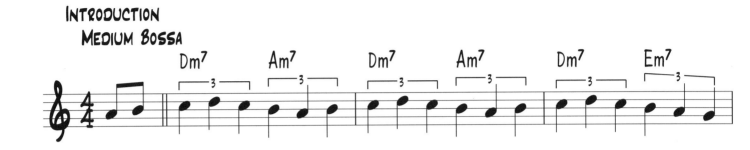

Flamingo

C VERSION

LYRIC BY ED ANDERSON
MUSIC BY TED GROUYA

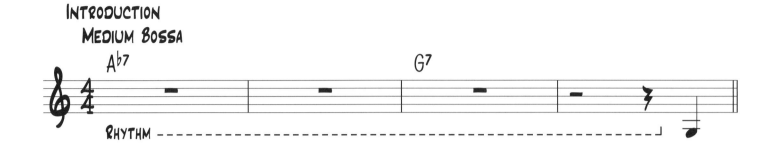

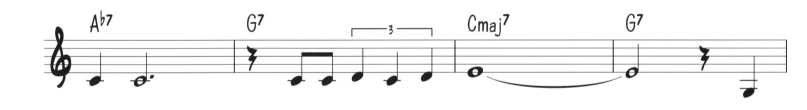

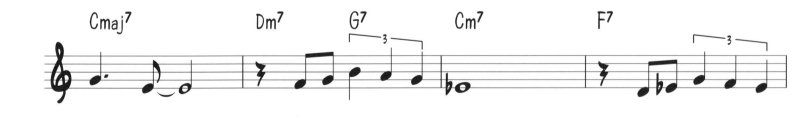

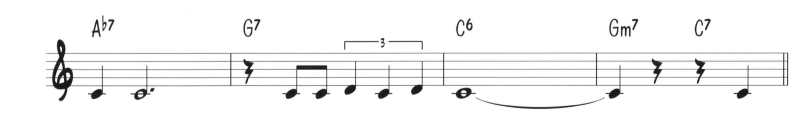

Gentle Rain

C Version

Music by Luiz Bonfa
Words by Matt Dubey

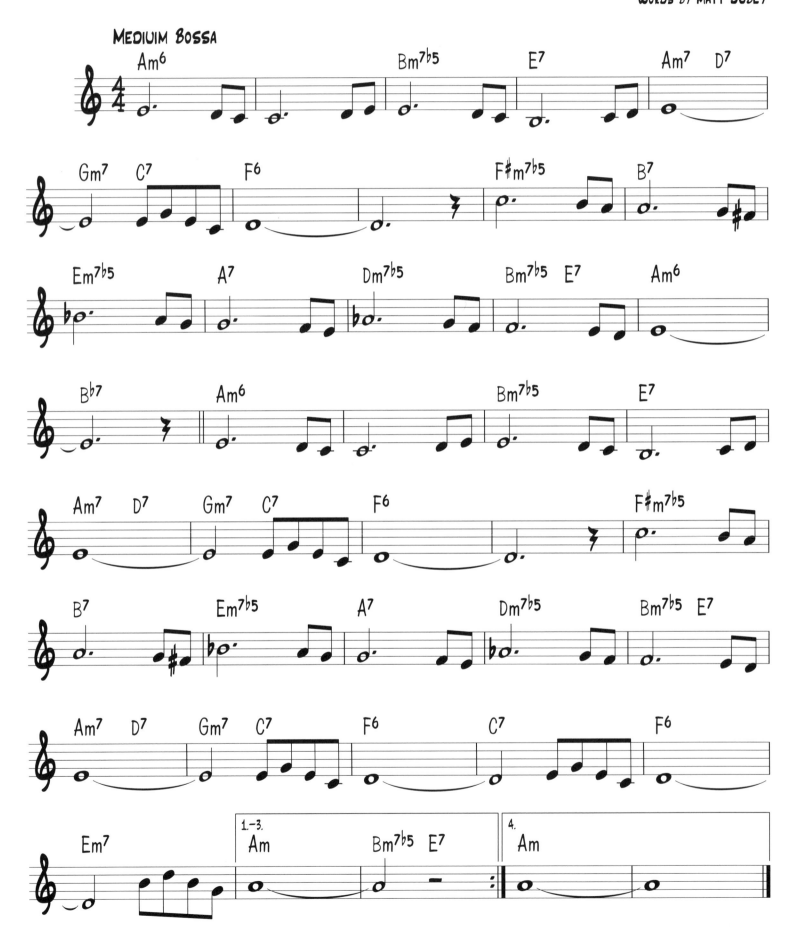

SAMBA DE ORFEU
(SAMBA DE ORPHEE)

By Luiz Bonfa

C Version

(*Cmaj7 second time)

THE GIFT!
(RECADO BOSSA NOVA)

C VERSION

MUSIC BY DJALMA FERREIRA
ORIGINAL LYRIC BY LUIZ ANTONIO
ENGLISH LYRIC BY PAUL FRANCIS WEBSTER

HOW INSENSITIVE
(Insensatéz)

C Version

Music by Antonio Carlos Jobim
Original Words by Vinicius de Moraes
English Words by Norman Gimbel

ONCE I LOVED
(Amor em Paz)
(Love in Peace)

C Version

Music by Antonio Carlos Jobim
Portuguese Lyrics by Vinicius de Maraes
English Lyrics by Ray Gilbert

Medium Bossa

Oye Como Va

C VERSION

WORDS AND MUSIC BY
TITO PUENTE

PETITE FLEUR

C VERSION

By Sidney Bechet

INTRODUCTION
SLOW BOSSA

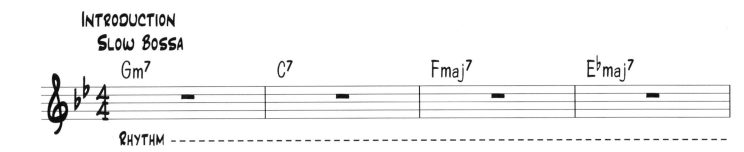

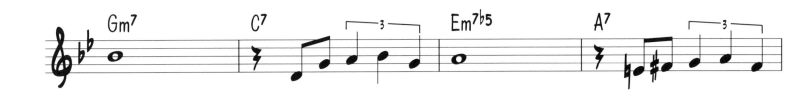

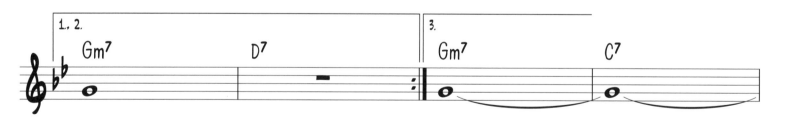

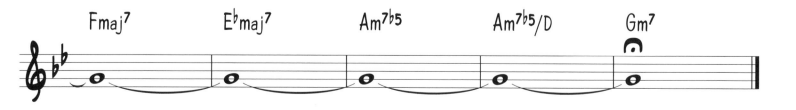

Só Danço Samba
(Jazz 'n' Samba)

C Version

Original Text by Vinicius de Moraes
Music by Antonio Carlos Jobim

INTRODUCTION
SAMBA

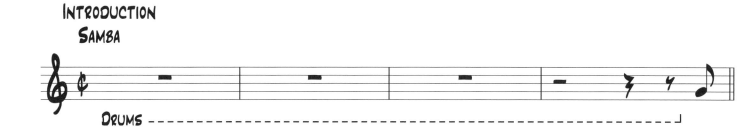

DRUMS –

So Nice
(Summer Samba)

C Version

Original Words and Music by Marcos Valle
and Paulo Sergio Valle
English Words by Norman Gimbel

Introduction
Medium Bossa

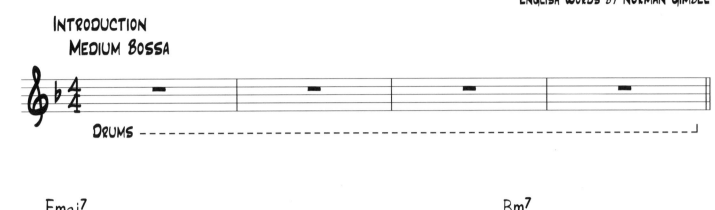

DRUMS

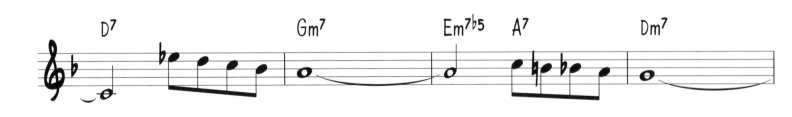

Song for My Father

C Version

Words and Music by
Horace Silver

Introduction
Medium Latin

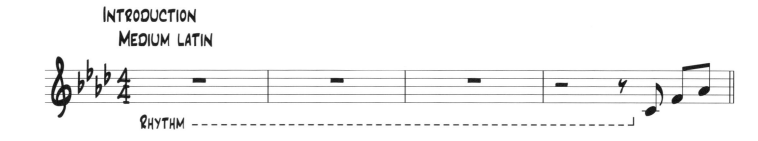

Rhythm -

Fm⁷

E♭⁷   D♭⁷

C⁷   Fm⁷

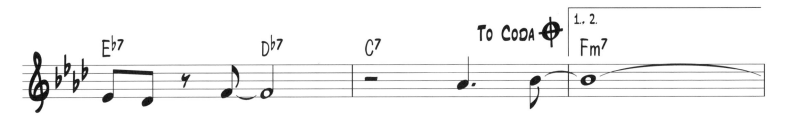

Sway
(Quien Será)

C Version

English Words by Norman Gimbel
Spanish Words and Music by Pablo Beltran Ruiz

TICO TICO
(TICO TICO NO FUBA)

C VERSION

Words and Music by ZEQUINHA ABREU,
ALOYSIO OLIVEIRA AND ERVIN DRAKE

WHATEVER LOLA WANTS
(Lola Gets)

C VERSION

Words and Music by Richard Adler
and Jerry Ross

Slow Hot Wind
(Lujon)

C Version

Words by Norman Gimbel
Music by Henry Mancini

BAIA
(BAHIA)

Bb VERSION

MUSIC AND PORTUGUESE LYRIC BY ARY BARROSO
ENGLISH LYRIC BY RAY GILBERT

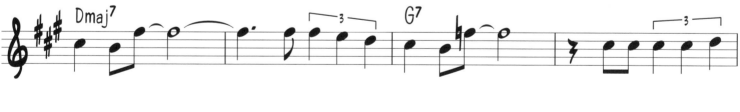

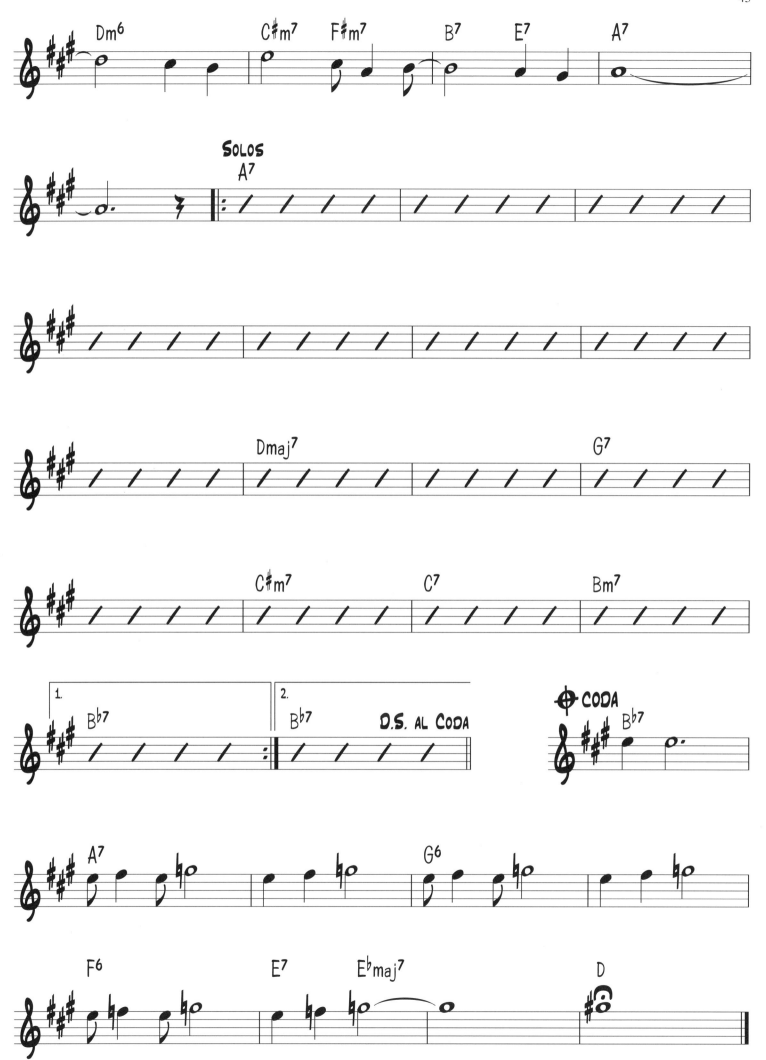

BEGIN THE BEGUINE

B♭ VERSION

WORDS AND MUSIC BY
COLE PORTER

Gentle Rain

8ᵇ Version

Music by Luiz Bonfa
Words by Matt Dubey

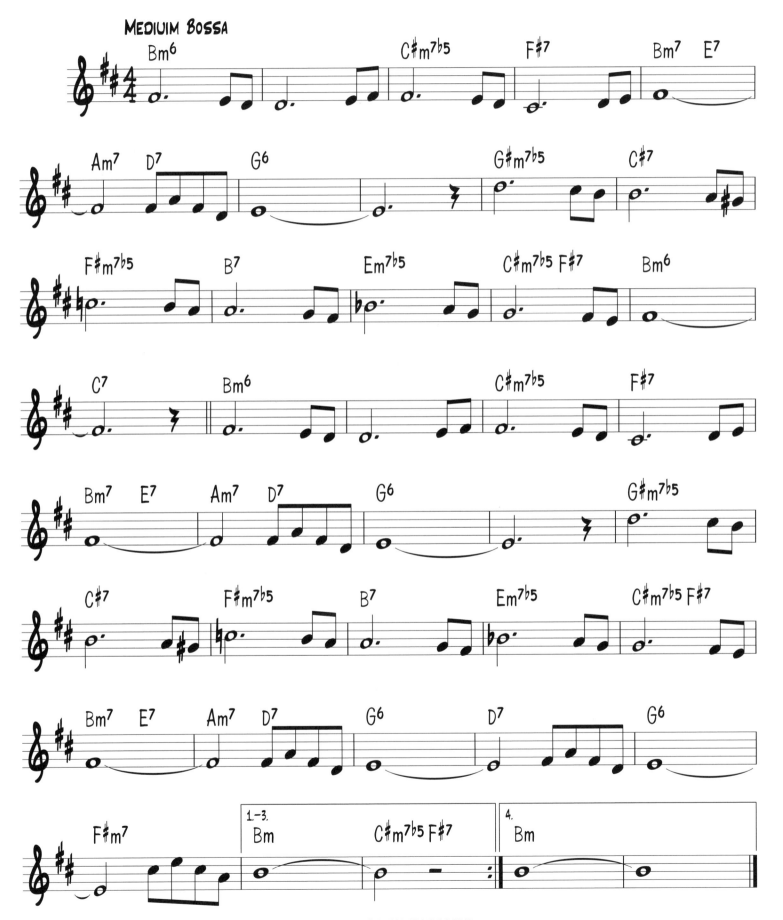

Black Orpheus

8ᵇ Version

Words and Music by Luiz Bonfa
and Antonio Carlos Jobim

**Introduction
Medium Bossa**

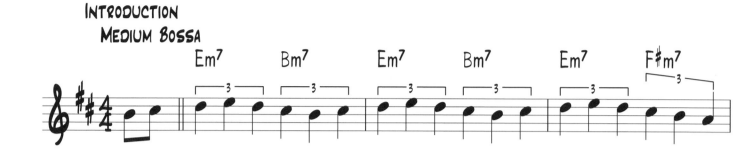

Flamingo

Bb Version

Lyric by Ed Anderson
Music by Ted Grouya

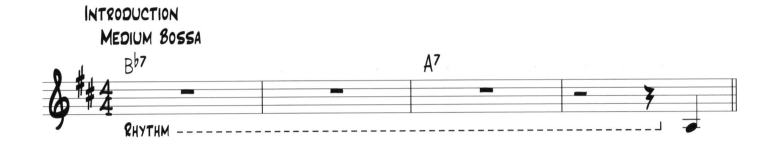

THE GIFT!
(Recado Bossa Nova)

B♭ Version

Music by Djalma Ferreira
Original Lyric by Luiz Antonio
English Lyric by Paul Francis Webster

How Insensitive
(Insensatéz)

8♭ Version

Music by Antonio Carlos Jobim
Original Words by Vinicius De Moraes
English Words by Norman Gimbel

ONCE I LOVED
(Amor em Paz)
(Love in Peace)

Bb Version

Music by Antonio Carlos Jobim
Portuguese Lyrics by Vinicius de Maraes
English Lyrics by Ray Gilbert

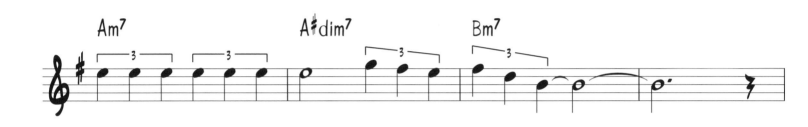

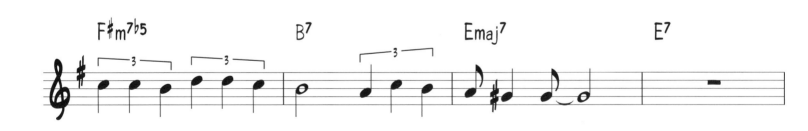

OYE COMO VA

8♭ Version

Words and Music by
Tito Puente

PETITE FLEUR

Bb Version

By Sidney Bechet

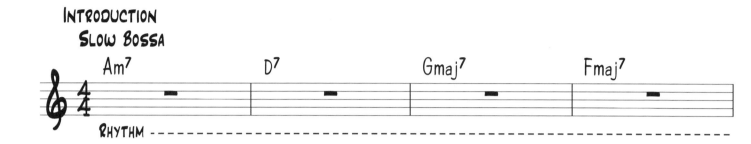

SAMBA DE ORFEU
(SAMBA DE ORPHEE)

Bᵇ VERSION

By LUIZ BONFA

(*Dmaj7 SECOND TIME)

64

Slow Hot Wind
(Lujon)

Bb Version

Words by Norman Gimbel
Music by Henry Mancini

Só Danço Samba
(Jazz 'n' Samba)

B♭ Version

Original Text by Vinicius de Moraes
Music by Antonio Carlos Jobim

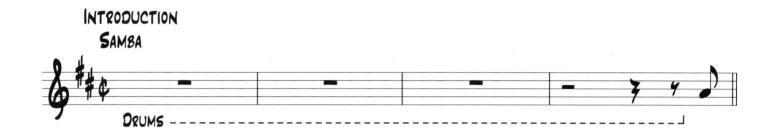

SO NICE
(Summer Samba)

Bb Version

Original Words and Music by Marcos Valle
and Paulo Sergio Valle
English Words by Norman Gimbel

Song for My Father

8♭ Version

Words and Music by
Horace Silver

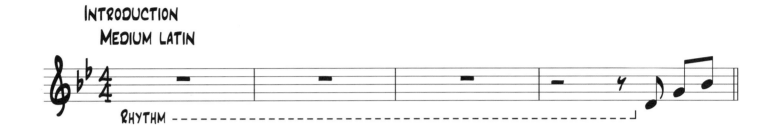

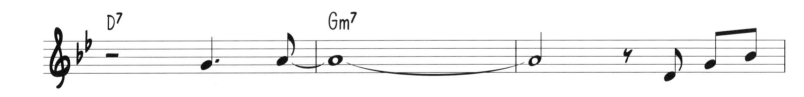

Sway
(Quien Será)

Bb Version

English Words by Norman Gimbel
Spanish Words and Music by Pablo Beltran Ruiz

TICO TICO
(TICO TICO NO FUBA)

Bb VERSION

WORDS AND MUSIC BY ZEQUINHA ABREU,
ALOYSIO OLIVEIRA AND ERVIN DRAKE

WHATEVER LOLA WANTS
(Lola Gets)

Bb Version

Words and Music by Richard Adler
and Jerry Ross

BAIA
(Bahia)

Eb VERSION

Music and Portuguese Lyric by ARY BARROSO
English Lyric by RAY GILBERT

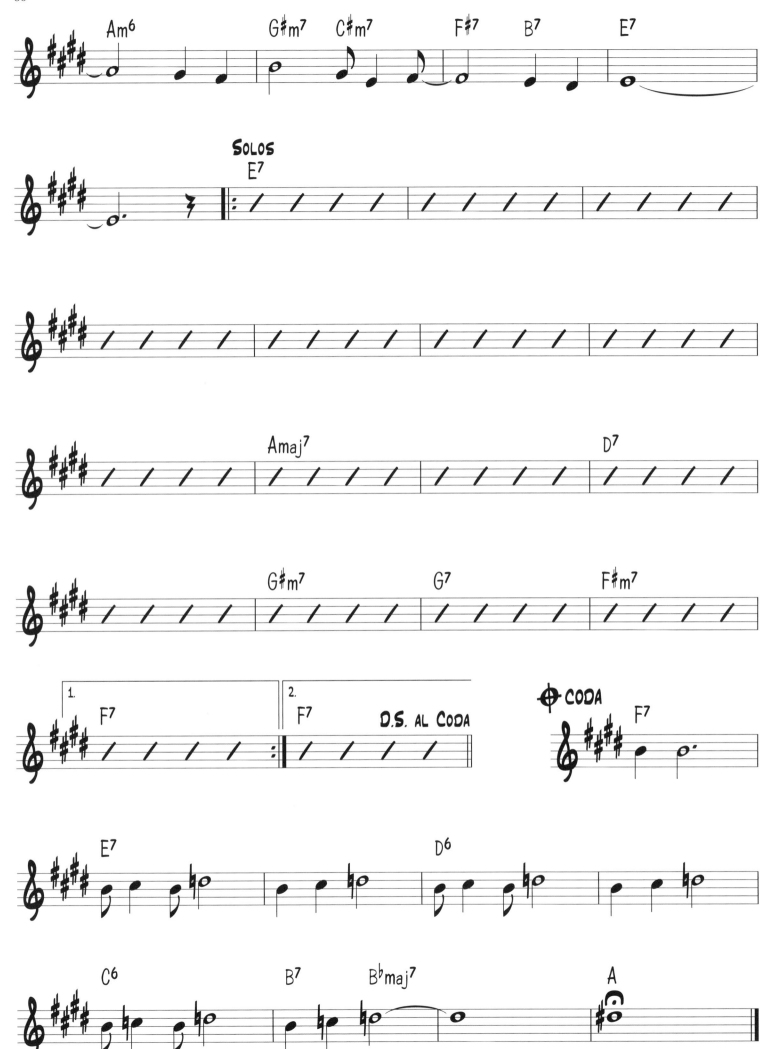

BEGIN THE BEGUINE

E♭ Version

Words and Music by
Cole Porter

Black Orpheus

Eb Version

Words and Music by Luiz Bonfa
and Antonio Carlos Jobim

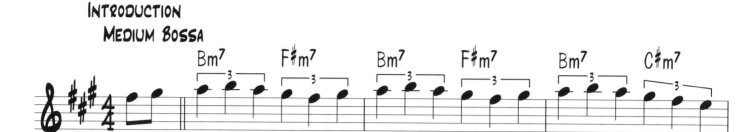

Flamingo

Eb Version

Lyric by Ed Anderson
Music by Ted Grouya

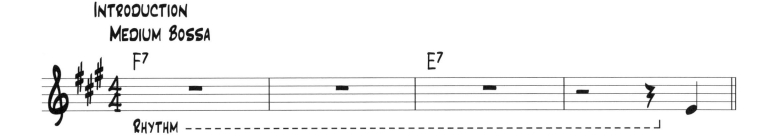

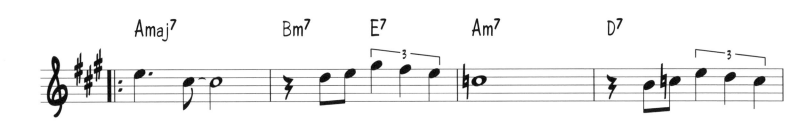

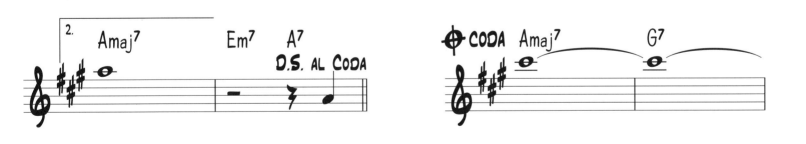

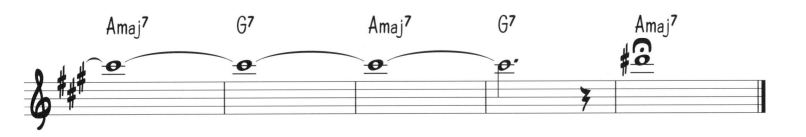

Gentle Rain

Eb Version

Music by Luiz Bonfa
Words by Matt Dubey

SAMBA DE ORFEU
(Samba de Orphee)

Eb Version

By Luiz Bonfa

(*Amaj7 second time)

THE GIFT!
(Recado Bossa Nova)

Eb Version

Music by Djalma Ferreira
Original Lyric by Luiz Antonio
English Lyric by Paul Francis Webster

How Insensitive
(Insensatez)

Eb Version

Music by Antonio Carlos Jobim
Original Words by Vinicius de Moraes
English Words by Norman Gimbel

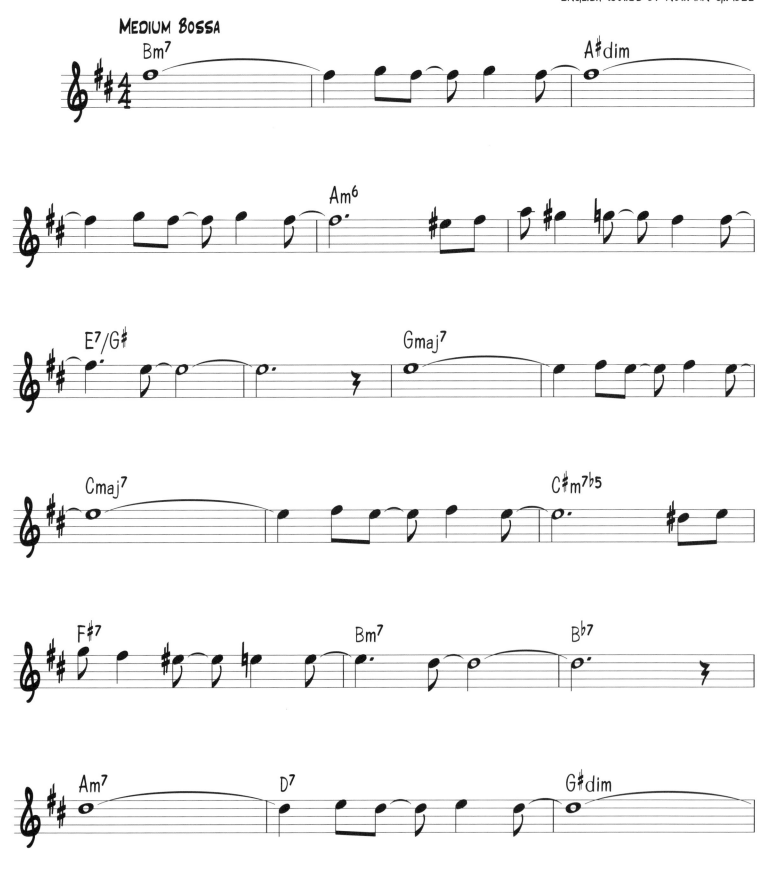

Once I Loved
(Amor em Paz)
(Love in Peace)

E♭ Version

Music by Antonio Carlos Jobim
Portuguese Lyrics by Vinicius de Maraes
English Lyrics by Ray Gilbert

OYE COMO VA

Eb VERSION

WORDS AND MUSIC BY
TITO PUENTE

Petite Fleur

E♭ Version

By Sidney Bechet

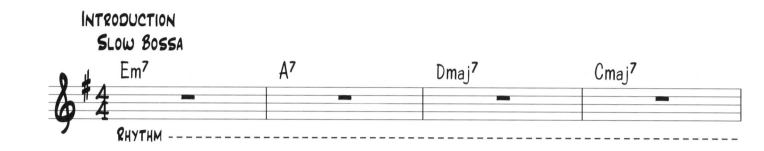

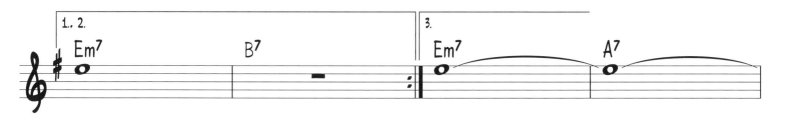

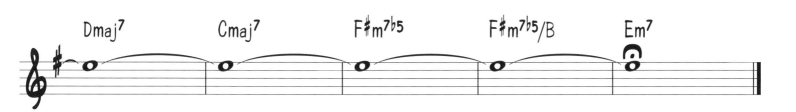

Só Danço Samba
(Jazz 'N' Samba)

Eb Version

Original Text by Vinicius de Moraes
Music by Antonio Carlos Jobim

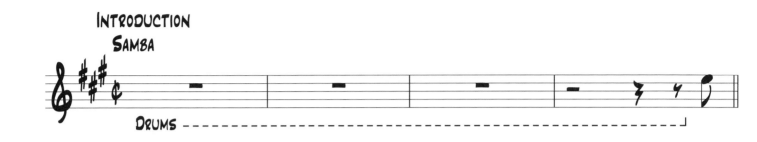

SO NICE
(Summer Samba)

Eb Version

Original Words and Music by Marcos Valle
and Paulo Sergio Valle
English Words by Norman Gimbel

Song for My Father

Eb Version

Words and Music by
Horace Silver

Introduction
Medium Latin

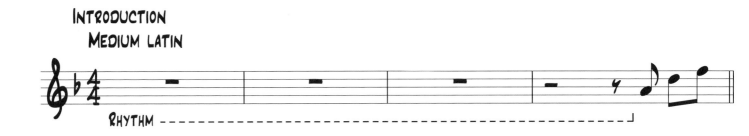

RHYTHM ------------------------------

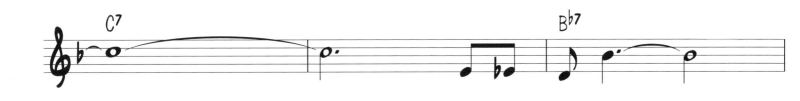

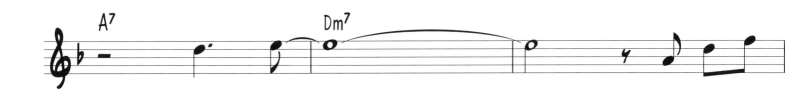

Sway
(Quien Será)

E♭ Version

English Words by Norman Gimbel
Spanish Words and Music by Pablo Beltran Ruiz

TICO TICO
(TICO TICO NO FUBA)

Eᵇ VERSION

WORDS AND MUSIC BY ZEQUINHA ABREU,
ALOYSIO OLIVEIRA AND ERVIN DRAKE

WHATEVER LOLA WANTS
(LOLA GETS)

Eb VERSION

WORDS AND MUSIC BY RICHARD ADLER
AND JERRY ROSS

Slow Hot Wind
(Lujon)

E♭ Version

Words by Norman Gimbel
Music by Henry Mancini

BAIA
(Bahia)

C VERSION

Music and Portuguese Lyric by Ary Barroso
English Lyric by Ray Gilbert

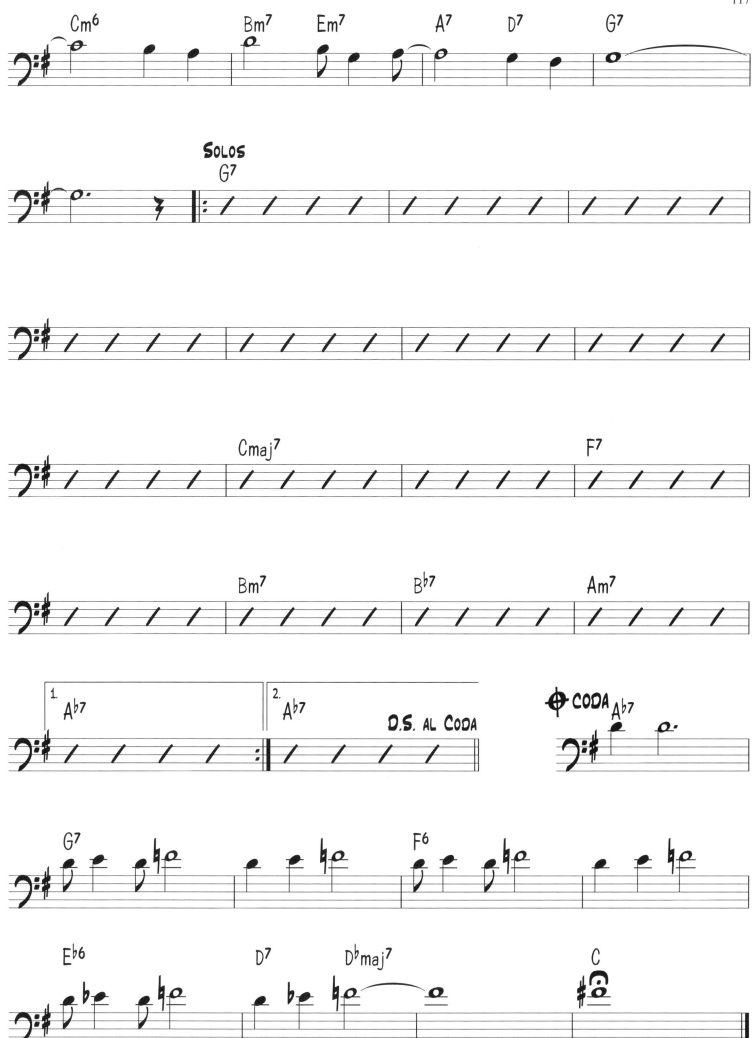

BEGIN THE BEGUINE

꜀: C Version

Words and Music by
Cole Porter

Medium Beguine

Gentle Rain

♭: C Version

Music by Luiz Bonfa
Words by Matt Dubey

Black Orpheus

𝄢 C Version

Words and Music by Luiz Bonfa
and Antonio Carlos Jobim

Introduction
Medium Bossa

Flamingo

⊃: C Version

Lyric by Ed Anderson
Music by Ted Grouya

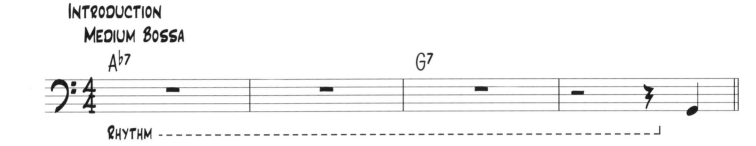

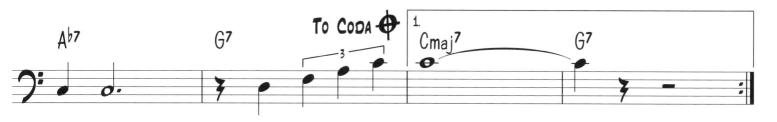

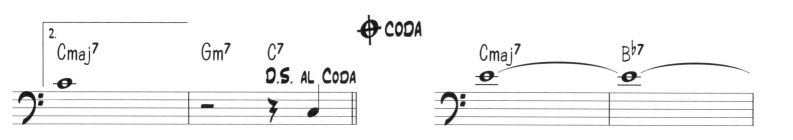

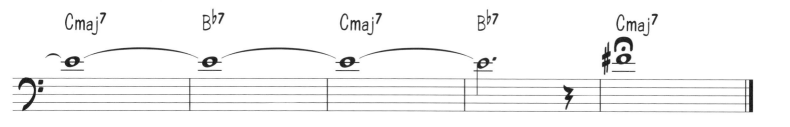

THE GIFT!
(Recado Bossa Nova)

C Version

Music by Djalma Ferreira
Original Lyric by Luiz Antonio
English Lyric by Paul Francis Webster

HOW INSENSITIVE
(INSENSATEZ)

: C VERSION

MUSIC BY ANTONIO CARLOS JOBIM
ORIGINAL WORDS BY VINICIUS DE MORAES
ENGLISH WORDS BY NORMAN GIMBEL

MEDIUM BOSSA

ONCE I LOVED
(AMOR EM PAZ)
(LOVE IN PEACE)

♭ C VERSION

Music by Antonio Carlos Jobim
Portuguese Lyrics by Vinicius de Moraes
English Lyrics by Ray Gilbert

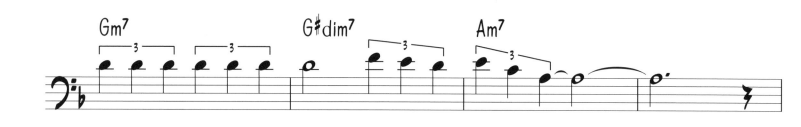

Oye Como Va

C Version

Words and Music by
Tito Puente

Petite Fleur

𝄢 C Version

By Sidney Bechet

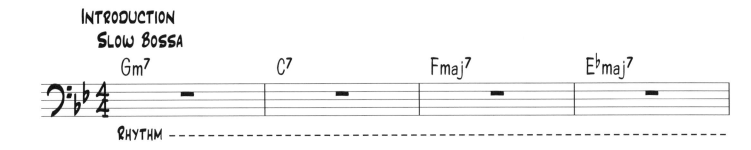

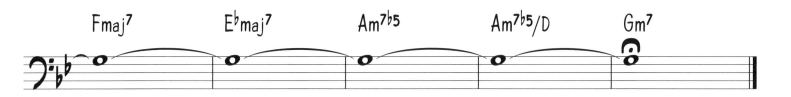

SAMBA DE ORFEU
(SAMBA DE ORPHEE)

C VERSION

By Luiz Bonfa

(*Cmaj7 second time)

Slow Hot Wind
(Lujon)

C Version

Words by Norman Gimbel
Music by Henry Mancini

SÓ DANÇO SAMBA
(JAZZ 'N' SAMBA)

C VERSION

ORIGINAL TEXT BY VINICIUS DE MORAES
MUSIC BY ANTONIO CARLOS JOBIM

INTRODUCTION
SAMBA

DRUMS

So Nice
(Summer Samba)

C Version

Original Words and Music by Marcos Valle
and Paulo Sergio Valle
English Words by Norman Gimbel

Introduction
Medium Bossa

Drums

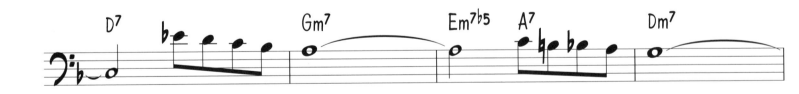

Song for My Father

𝄢 C Version

Words and Music by
Horace Silver

INTRODUCTION
MEDIUM LATIN

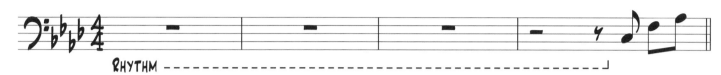

RHYTHM

Fm⁷ ... Eᵇ⁷ ... Dᵇ⁷

C⁷ ... Fm⁷

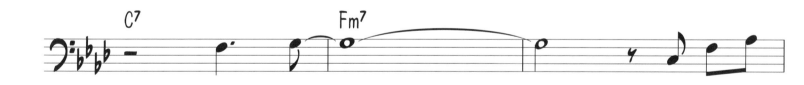

SWAY
(Quien Será)

C VERSION

English Words by Norman Gimbel
Spanish Words and Music by Pablo Beltran Ruiz

TICO TICO
(TICO TICO NO FUBA)

9: C VERSION

WORDS AND MUSIC BY ZEQUINHA ABREU,
ALOYSIO OLIVEIRA AND ERVIN DRAKE

WHATEVER LOLA WANTS
(Lola Gets)

C Version

Words and Music by Richard Adler
and Jerry Ross

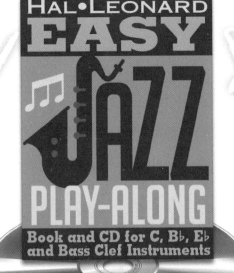

HAL•LEONARD EASY Jazz PLAY-ALONG

Book and CD for C, B♭, E♭ and Bass Clef Instruments

IMPROVISING IS EASIER THAN EVER

with this new series for beginning jazz musicians. The Hal Leonard Easy Jazz Play-Along Series includes songs with accessible chord changes and features recordings with novice-friendly tempos. Just follow the streamlined lead sheets in the book and play along with the professionally recorded backing tracks on the CD. The audio CD is playable on any CD player. For PC and Mac computer users, the CD is enhanced so you can adjust the recording to any tempo without changing pitch!

1. FIRST JAZZ SONGS
Book/CD Pack

All of Me • All the Things You Are • Autumn Leaves • C-Jam Blues • Comin' Home Baby • Footprints • The Girl from Ipanema (Garôta De Ipanema) • Killer Joe • Little Sunflower • Milestones • Mr. P.C. • On Green Dolphin Street • One for Daddy-O • Reunion Blues • Satin Doll • There Will Never Be Another You • Tune Up • Watermelon Man.

00843225 B♭, E♭, C & Bass Clef Instruments $19.99

2. STANDARDS FOR STARTERS
Book/CD Pack

Don't Get Around Much Anymore • Exactly like You • Fly Me to the Moon (In Other Words) • Have You Met Miss Jones? • Honeysuckle Rose • I Remember You • If I Should Lose You • It Could Happen to You • Moon River • My Favorite Things • On a Slow Boat to China • Out of Nowhere • Softly As in a Morning Sunrise • Speak Low • The Very Thought of You • Watch What Happens • The Way You Look Tonight • Yesterdays.

00843226 B♭, E♭, C & Bass Clef Instruments $19.99

3. EASY JAZZ CLASSICS
Book/CD Pack

Afternoon in Paris • Doxy • 500 Miles High • Girl Talk • Holy Land • Impressions • In Walked Bud • The Jive Samba • Lady Bird • Maiden Voyage • Mercy, Mercy, Mercy • My Little Suede Shoes • Recorda-Me • St. Thomas • Solar • Song for My Father • Stolen Moments • Sunny.

00843227 B♭, E♭, C & Bass Clef Instruments $19.99

4. BASIC BLUES
Book/CD Pack

All Blues • Birk's Works • Bloomdido • Blue Seven • Blue Train (Blue Trane) • Blues in the Closet • Cousin Mary • Freddie Freeloader • The Jody Grind • Jumpin' with Symphony Sid • Nostalgia in Times Square • Now See How You Are • Now's the Time • Sonnymoon for Two • Tenor Madness • Things Ain't What They Used to Be • Turnaround • Two Degrees East, Three Degrees West.

00843228 B♭, E♭, C & Bass Clef Instruments $19.99

5. EASY LATIN CLASSICS
Book/CD Pack

Baia (Bahía) • Begin the Beguine • Black Orpheus • Flamingo • Gentle Rain • The Gift! (Recado Bossa Nova) • How Insensitive (Insensatez) • Once I Loved (Amor Em Paz) (Love in Peace) • Oye Como Va • Petite Fleur (Little Flower) • Slow Hot Wind (Lujon) • Só Danço Samba (Jazz 'N' Samba) • So Nice (Summer Samba) • Song for My Father • Sway (Quien Sera) • Sweet Happy Life (Samba de Orpheo) • Tico Tico (Tico Tico No Fuba) • Whatever Lola Wants.

00843242 B♭, E♭, C & Bass Clef Instruments $19.99

6. CHRISTMAS STANDARDS
Book/CD Pack

All I Want for Christmas Is My Two Front Teeth • Blue Christmas • Christmas Time Is Here • Do You Hear What I Hear • Feliz Navidad • Happy Holiday • Have Yourself a Merry Little Christmas • Here Comes Santa Claus (Right down Santa Claus Lane) • A Holly Jolly Christmas • I Saw Mommy Kissing Santa Claus • I'll Be Home for Christmas • Jingle-Bell Rock • Let It Snow! Let It Snow! Let It Snow! • Rudolph the Red-Nosed Reindeer • Santa Claus Is Comin' to Town • Silver and Gold • Silver Bells • Winter Wonderland.

00101397 B♭, E♭, C & Bass Clef Instruments $19.99

HAL•LEONARD® CORPORATION

7777 W. BLUEMOUND RD. P.O. BOX 13819 MILWAUKEE, WI 53213

Prices, content, and availability subject to change without notice.

0812